IN THE FEVER OF LOVE

Here is Solomon's bed,
Surrounded by sixty warriors,
The heroes of Israel. —Songs 3:7

IN THE FEVER OF LOVE

An Illumination of the Song of Songs

Rabbi Shefa Gold

Illustrations by Phillip Ratner
Courtesy of the Dennis & Phillip Ratner Museum
and the Israel Bible Museum Collection

Ben Yehuda Press
Teaneck, New Jersey

Published by Ben Yehuda Press
430 Kensington Road
Teaneck, NJ 07666

http://www.BenYehudaPress.com

Ben Yehuda Press books may be purchased for educational,
business or sales promotional use. For information, please
contact:
Special Markets, Ben Yehuda Press,
430 Kensington Road, Teaneck, NJ 07666.
markets@BenYehudaPress.com

hc ISBN   1-934730-25-4
hc ISBN13 978-1-934730-25-6

pb ISBN   1-934730-26-2
pb ISBN13 978-1-934730-26-3

Library of Congress Cataloging-in-Publication Data

Gold, Shefa.
 In the fever of love : an illumination of the Song of songs / Shefa
Gold ; illustrations by Philip [sic.] Ratner.
    p. cm.
 ISBN 978-1-934730-25-6 (hardcover) – ISBN
978-1-934730-26-3 (pbk.)
  1. Bible. O.T. Song of Solomon–Commentaries. I. Ratner, Phil.
II. Bible. O.T. Song of Solomon. English. Gold. 2009. III. Title.

 BS1485.3.G63 2009
 223'.9077–dc22

                              2008049695

09 10 / 10 9 8 7 6 5 4 3 2

This book is dedicated
to my husband, friend,
beloved, partner, spirit-buddy…
Rachmiel,
who keeps me honest,
who forgives me my eccentricities,
inviting and receiving my deepest, sweetest intentions
for Love;
who holds me in a wide and cherishing embrace,
and loves me so well.

And to lovers everywhere.

Contents

Foreword by
The Rev. Robert Corin Morris

You don't have to be a mystic to enjoy Rabbi Shefa Gold's new commentary on the Song of Songs, but it may make you into one. Rather than address herself to the reader, she speaks directly, and passionately, to God, The Beloved. She invites us to share in her conversation with life itself, with the mystery that wells "at the center of every molecule, at the heart of my being." This book breathes new life into the ancient practice of both Jews and Christians to read the Song as an allegory of the love between God and human beings.

Some mystical teaching takes us away from this world. Shefa belongs to that deeper stream that invites us to plunge into the heart of ordinary life and find the Holy there. Ordinary love becomes a primary doorway to the God who says, "Choose life" as it is, not as we might like it to be. Everyday experience becomes the winnowing, purifying path beyond the ego's defensive isolation into our deepest capacities for love and right relationship.

The rich, poetic text can be used for pondering, praying, and perceiving life in a deeper way by people of any faith, but remains deeply rooted in Judaism's down-to-earth approach to the world.

Shefa brings a modern psychological awareness to this ancient text, which values as "grist for the mill" not only the virtues, but also the shadow side of our soul. Our passion to be "fully ourselves" and "live life to the full" is claimed as a doorway into God, if we can but see that, in all things, God is seeking to embrace us more fully. "How shall I embrace this life that I have been given?" she asks. The answer? Embrace life fully, both the light and the dark.

In interpreting "I am dark and beautiful," for example, she includes our mistakes, regrets, our quarrel with life and argument with the world. Even in these, "dark beauty" shines. What could be truer to the tradition of Jacob/Israel, who wrestled in the dark with a stranger who turned out to be God. The "wilderness" of the text becomes the modern wilderness of aloneness. The "garden" becomes the totality of life, "both its awesomeness and its awfulness, all of it." "Sleep" becomes our media-driven, trance-like conformity. What is essential—and this has always been the mystic's message—is to find in the midst of life's tumult "a center of calm, my still and spacious, waiting, open heart." Only from this place can the Beloved's hidden presence become manifest.

For those who want specific directions, she appends ten "commandments" from the Song (actually, twenty, since each is bi-partate) which can be maxims for daily living.

The Rev. Robert Corin Morris,
Episcopal Priest,
Executive Director of Interweave,
author of *Wrestling with Grace*
and *Suffering and the Courage of God.*

Introduction:
Initiation onto the Path of Love

"The whole Torah is Holy," says Rabbi Akiva, "but the Song of Songs is the Holy of Holies."[*]

When it came time to decide which of the ancient books would become part of the canon for Israel, there was a stormy argument about this beloved text, sometimes called "The Song of Solomon."

The objections were numerous:

The name of God is absent from its pages; its words were lustily sung in every tavern. Not only does it glorify sexual love but the lovers were clearly not married! Further, it celebrates Nature and the pleasures of the body.

Yet, despite all these arguments, the opinion of Rabbi Akiva (a great mystic and an important religious leader in the 2nd century) held sway, and the Song of Songs was preserved as one of the holy books of Torah.

Judaism is a great storehouse of treasures. And it is a vital, dynamic, living conversation that spans the globe and the centuries. Every generation inherits the accumulation of text, music, commentary, law, custom, recipes, and secret wisdom. And it is the responsibility of each generation to experience revelation: to fully receive, interpret, and add to the treasure. Further, we are charged to pass it on to the generation to come—in a form more relevant and more alive to our present-day challenges and sensibilities. In this way, the storehouse is constantly renewed, and will stand for all time, a witness to everything that has passed before and a

---

[*] Mishnah Yadayyim 3:5

guide to what comes next.

The Torah commands that we love God "with all our heart, with all our soul and with all our might." We are commanded to "love the stranger" and "to love our neighbor as our own selves." And we are asked to receive God's love in the form of Torah, community, history and the wonders of Nature. These commandments *to love* are at the heart of Torah. They constitute the most simple, and the most complicated, challenge to living a holy life.

The Path of Love is the attempt to meet the challenge of learning to love and be loved. It is the most rigorous spiritual path of all.

Stepping onto the Path of Love, I am faced with every resistance, every illusion, every obstacle to self-realization. The Great Work is suddenly laid out before me in startling detail. In the words of the Song, "I was asleep but my heart was awake. Listen! My lover is knocking."

The Song sings to all whose hearts lie awake, waiting to be roused by God, our true love, Who is knocking and Who calls us to become ourselves and to be connected in sacred union with all of Creation and with the Source of All. God is knocking with the reality of each moment. I am not always open to hearing the call: Sometimes the truth of this moment is distorted when desire compels me to reach out for what's next and thus miss what is right in front of me; or when I am so preoccupied with the past or my ideas about what *should* be, that I miss what *is*.

My initiation onto this Path of Love requires that I wake up and stay present to the truth that is spread before me, to the miraculous garden of my ongoing re-birth. It requires that I open my heart to the "Other." It demands that I acknowledge and face squarely every obstacle to love's fulfillment. Those obstacles are my defenses, built by the false self out of layers of fear and the illusion of my separateness from God and Creation.

One year I sat around a table at a Passover Seder with a group of women. It was during the war in Bosnia and we all felt helpless, knowing that the tragedy of genocide was unfolding while the world stood by. As Jews, imprinted with the history of the Holocaust, we felt particular despair. As we re-counted the foundational story of our people, the Exodus from Egypt, we were sensitive to its violence, the suffering of all those Egyptians from the plagues and the tragedy of their final drowning in the sea. Someone asked, "Don't we have any *other* story? Whenever *we* win, someone else loses. Do we always have to win our freedom at the expense of another people?" We were all reminded of the same tragedy playing itself out in the Middle East in which both Israelis and Palestinians claim their autonomy at the expense of the other, where one people's victory necessarily means the other's defeat. "Isn't there any other path to Freedom?" we asked. "Don't we have any *other* story?" As this question hung in the air between us, the silence felt like a great weight, and then an answer dawned.

"We *do* have another story!" I shouted. I explained that the Tradition calls us to read and study and sing the Song of Songs during Passover. While the Book of Exodus tells the story of our outer journey from slavery to freedom, the Song of Songs tells the inner story. Rabbi Akiva hinted at this when he called the Song "the Holy of Holies." Just as the Holy of Holies occupied the very center of the Sanctuary, the Song of Songs stands at the center of the mystery of

Freedom.

Freedom in our tradition is not merely a "freedom from"—from oppression, suffering, or servitude; it is a "freedom to"—to be in direct relationship with God our liberator. God says: I brought you out of Egypt to be your God, to be in relationship with you. It is this relationship that makes us free. The moment we cut ourselves off from God, we are back in Egypt; back in our chains of slavery.

The Song of Songs tells the story of relationship—its yearnings and heartbreaks, as well as its triumphs and pleasures. It shouts the glories of love and whispers its secrets. I move easily from the relationship of a people with their God to the complex web of relationship in my life. The Song sends me on the spiritual path of relationship. In relationship, all my ideals are tested and I am shown the places of my own fear, immaturity, impatience, pride and bitterness. Intimate relationship reveals to me where I still need work and healing. And it calls forth my greatest courage and love. My absolute best and worst character traits are made clearly visible in the practice of relationship, as well as a vision of what is possible if I open to the Great Love.

As I enter into the Song of Songs, I am tending the garden of two relationships at once—with my beloved partner in life and with God. These two relationships are in relationship with each other; they depend upon each other for their strength and stability. Shortly after my husband, Rachmiel, and I fell in love, he said to me, "I'm so glad that you love God more than you love me." He could feel that my love for God was a deep pool, a resource from which *all* my love flowed. He also knew that my relationship with God

Shefa Gold

meant that I wouldn't be expecting anything from him that only the Divine could give me. And Rachmiel was right. My connection to God is the foundation of my life. It waters the garden from which all my relationships grow.

As my marriage to Rachmiel grows, I begin to see how this human relationship refines my ability to give and receive, purifies my intentions, opens me to hard truths about myself. The fire of this relationship gives me the strength to stand before God in humility and express my true passion.

As I grow in these two relationships I sometimes get glimpses of the mystery of Love itself. Sometimes, Rachmiel and I disappear and there is only Love. Sometimes, God and I disappear and there is only Love. These glimpses appear only when I have surrendered myself totally. The path that the Song of Songs shows me is the path of complete embodiment. *Thinking* about love will not reveal its mysteries; we must enter through the senses, get our feet dirty, express our passionate longings, and breathe in the fragrances that surround us.

The Song of Songs urges us to go outside; search out the wildflowers, listen for the message of the dove and the nightingale, learn from the gazelle and the wild stag. My initiation onto the Path of Love moves me beyond mere comfort and convenience, and leads me to perceive the wisdom and Grace of Nature. Only then can I discover that same wild grace in my own body. My initiation is an invitation to fully inhabit my body, explore its capacity for pleasure, and feel in tune with the rhythms and cycles of Nature.

The truth of my spiritual life is that I encounter God

the most clearly in these three ways: through my body and its expanding senses, through Nature and its dramatic and miraculous beauty, and through intimacy with the Other. The Song of Songs provides me with the language to talk about these three ways of encounter. Its language connects me with my ancestors who opened the same doors, walked the same path, and were initiated into the mysteries of Love.

In the next section you will find the original text of The Song of Songs (my translation from the Hebrew), followed by my response. I recommend that you find someone to read it to, and do so aloud in your most loving voice.

This is what I call a "devotional" commentary. Rather than talk about the text, I enter through the door that is opened by these ancient words. Once through that door, I can sing to God, "Oh, give me the kisses of your mouth, for your sweet loving is better than wine."

When I fell in love with this "sweet loving" of the Song of Songs, I hired a scribe to create a scroll for me with the Hebrew text of Shir HaShirim, and I prayed from it each morning. I found myself very inspired by a teaching of Rabbi Akiva's that "Had the Torah not been given, we could live our lives by the Song of Songs." Each day for a year and a half, I chanted The Song and held in my heart the question, "What would it mean to live my life by this?" The last section of this book, The Ten Commandments of The Song of Songs, is my attempt to answer that question.

As a passionate mystic-activist my intention is to return this sacred erotic text to its rightful place at the center of our religious lives. The Song of Songs is an invitation to enter the Holy of Holies at the center of our own loving

Shefa Gold

hearts. When we take that journey to Center and finally turn towards the shining face of The One who has been waiting there, then every facet of our lives begins to shine with the beauty of The Beloved.

A Devotional Commentary

I read every word of "The Song" as a word that I address
to God my Beloved AND as a word that is addressed
to me by God. Each word of the Song is also the word
that I address to my lover AND each word is spoken
by my lover to me. Love is given and received at once.
If the *Song of Songs* is a story, then it is the kind of
story where the end suffuses the beginning and the
beginning echoes the end. This story takes place in a
Timeless Time, forever beginning, forever unfolding,
forever ending.

I am indebted to those who have analyzed, sung, lived,
studied and translated this sacred text and have
bequeathed to me their wisdom and insights. My own
translation has been informed and enriched by the
translations and interpretations of Ariel and Chana
Bloch, Marcia Falk, Marvin Pope, Philip Birnbaum,
The ArtScroll allegorical rendering following Rashi,
The Jerusalem Bible, The New JPS Translation, and
Midrash Rabbah.

I feel blessed by Phillip Ratner's generosity in allowing his
pictures to grace this text.

Note: My translation of the text of the Song is in *italic
bold*. My commentary follows in plain type.

Oh, give me the kisses of your mouth,
For your sweet loving is better than wine. — Songs 1:2

1. A Call to Intimacy

Oh, give me the kisses of your mouth,
For your sweet loving is better than wine,

I am called to intimacy, and my longing calls me to Life.
  I request Your mouth; I invite the Supreme Risk.
  Your kiss is Death as well as Revelation. Yet I know
  that all the wine I have drunk is just a taste; each and
  every moment of ecstasy only stirs the coals. A spark,
  my true spark, awakens, leaps and then grows dark
  again. Each time I feel Your breath on my face, my
  spark awakens and twinkles with laughter or trembles
  with terror. And then, I am all lips, all expectancy, all
  hunger.

Your juices are fragrant,
Your essence pours out like oil,
This is why all the young women want you.

Take me with you, let us run together!

Your fragrance, the scent of Reality, lures me
Beneath the dry surface of this seeming world...
Behind the shadows that confound me...
Between the sureties of conception and form
The tantalizing fragrance of Your Presence calls to me.

You long for me as I long for You,
You defy description and elude my grasp,

Yet as Your Essence pours into this world,
All forms are moistened with mystery.

Your Essence pours into my body and I become fluid.
Dancing wildly, I recover my full range of emotion,
I am infused with desire.

The King has brought me to his chambers.
Let us delight and rejoice in your love,
Enjoying each caress more than wine,
They are right to love you so.

I love You
   with all my heart   all my soul   all my might.

As I pass through, these words call from every doorway,
But I do not calmly walk into your chambers;
   I am brought,
Sometimes dragged—kicking, struggling, screaming.

Only after my heart's been broken,
  My will defeated,
    My expectations deflated,
Only now is true delight born. Only now
Does inner joy shine through outer circumstance.

This joy is delight in Being,
This love is existence itself.
Each breath touches my insides as a caress
Both soothing and arousing.

I am dark and beautiful, Oh Daughters of Jerusalem,
Dark as the tents of Kedar, lavish as Solomon's
    tapestries,
Do not see me only as dark
For the sun has stared at me.
My brothers quarreled with me;
They made me guard the vineyard.
I have not guarded my own.

My dark beauty shines in the life that I have lived, the
    mistakes that I have made. This dark beauty shines in
    my regrets, in the tears that I have shed for love lost. I
    have been weathered. Each wrinkle on my face shows a
    road on the map. And the circuitous journey is etched
    on my soul. Yet my darkness is still a mystery which I
    offer up to the fires of awareness. I have quarreled with
    my life. My argument with the World is exhausting.
    Yet you see me. You harvest the fruit of my unguarded
    vineyard. I open the gate wide and wider still, to
    receive You.

Tell me, my only love,
Where do you pasture your sheep,
Where do you rest them in the heat of noon?
Why should I wander among the flocks of your
    companions?

Why should I waste my time on anything less than our
    moments together? Why do I squander my time in
    worry, regret, scheming, blame or recrimination? It is
    Your Presence that nourishes and fills me;

Your Light that illuminates and dazzles me;
Your Warmth that comforts me.

Loveliest of women,
If you wander,
Follow in the tracks of the sheep,
Graze your goats in the shadow of the shepherd's
tents,

As I wander and stumble upon hidden pathways,
I begin to listen to my body's message
Urging me towards balance, vitality and wholeness.

My animal holiness signals with each moment—
An explosion of impulse. As I purify this impulse and
listen
Ever more carefully to its nuanced truth,
I cultivate the courage to follow
And obey.... The body doesn't lie.
My obedience is to this truth—
A Divine voice speaking through Existence.

I see you, my love, as a mare,
Among Pharoah's chariots.

My love is the wild-in-me that is harnessed to the chariot
of Truth, yet never tamed. My love is gentle, yet more
powerful than an army. My love is mystery unfolding
infinitely.

I see you, my love, as a mare,
Among Pharoah's chariots. — Songs 1:9

הִנָּךְ יָפָה רַעְיָתִי הִנָּךְ יָפָה עֵינַיִךְ יוֹנִים׃

*How beautiful you are, my friend,
Your eyes are doves. — Songs 1:15*

Shefa Gold

Your cheeks as beautiful as jewels,
Your throat encircled with beads,
I will make you golden earrings studded with silver.

I receive my Life plain, unadorned,
And then pleasure stirs. With my laughter,
With my fanciful story, through the prism of my joy
This world is made precious,
The light from within shines out as sparkle,
Luring me within and beyond.

When the King lay down beside me,
My perfume gave forth its sweetness.
All night my beloved sleeps between my breasts,
A cluster of myrrh,
A spray of henna blossoms,
from the vineyards of Ein Gedi.

Only in Your Presence is my true fragrance revealed.
My perfume is complex—a note of sweetness, yes...
But also terror, anguish, absurd humor, surprise
And a musky gratefulness for Life.

My fragrance mingles with the night,
We are drunk with it.

How beautiful you are, my friend,
Your eyes are doves.
And how beautiful you are, my beloved,
And how gentle,

Wherever we lie, our bed is green,
Our roofbeams are cedar, our rafters, fir.

The eyes of my heart have wings. I open my heart's eyes
To lift myself above the clouds of confusion,
That I might see wide and clear
The beauty that's before me. In this moment
I fall fiercely in love with my life, knowing in my heart…
Wherever I step, wherever I sit, wherever I lie
        You are beside me
        Embracing me
        Urging me on.

2. Surprise Me
on the Jagged Mountain

I am the rose of Sharon
A lily of the valleys.

I flower: bursting with color, vibrancy and proud seed, I
announce my life to the world. So very bold! And yet
vulnerable to each passing breeze, each mood, each
day's surprise. Attentive to this patch of ground, I put
forth my tendrils, encountering rich soil, immovable
rock. I root myself in the earth of this life, this family,
these circumstances—while knowing how fragile is my
certainty, how delicate my identity.

Like a lily among the thorns,
So is my beloved among the young women.

And my beloved among the young men is
Like an apple tree among the trees of the wood.
In that shade I delight to sit
Tasting his sweet fruit.

The garden of my heart is surrounded by wilderness,
A treasure hidden by thick brambles and scrub-oaks
Whose roots spread with vicious intensity,
Blocking the paths, and yet…
I can smell that lily, that apple-blossom shimmering
At the center of my heart, its fragrance calling me.

Like a lily among the thorns,
So is my beloved among the young women. —Songs 2:2

In my frustration I struggle to reach it. But when I stop
And sit and sigh and finally come to stillness... suddenly
I am resting in Your shade.
The taste of Your sweet fruit fulfills me.

Looking out from the center of this garden,
Even my thorny life
Makes perfect sense.

He brought me to the tavern,
And his banner over me is Love.

I am brought to the "tavern"
Against my small will,
My will to stay separate, distinct from the cosmos.

There is yet a larger force within me,
A larger Knowing that connects my Self
To the farthest star; I am a microcosm of the Universe.
It is that Will that binds my spirit
Dragging me to the "tavern," where I become intoxicated,
Where I can finally surrender.

In the "tavern" I am claimed by Love.
There "I" am finally defeated. Yet in this defeat,
    I am ravished;
God finds victory within me.

Cover me with blossoms,
Refresh me with apples
For I am in the fever of Love.

His left hand beneath my head,
His right arm embracing me.

What looks like sickness is true health. What passes for
    brokenness is only the path to my wholeness, the place
    where passion burns like the burning bush, with flames
    that don't consume, but give life with every spark.
    When I surrender to the "fever of love"; when I consent
    to the embrace of My Lover; when I stop resisting and
    instead rest, lean into those arms that support me… I
    am held in the contours of Life. Then, unafraid, I can
    eat from the Original Tree and share its fruit with
    every hungry, curious Adam, every searching, thirsting
    Eve. This fever is the sun at the center of my heart,
    shining out, ripening the fruit that is me.

Daughters of Jerusalem, swear to me
By the gazelles, by the deer in the field,
That you will not awaken Love until it is ripe.

Friends of my soul, I ask you this:
Be my witness, my companion in abandon,
See in the tight bud, my blossoming beauty,
    have patience for the deepening of color,
    the ripening of friendship,
For Love awakening in its time.

My beloved among the young men is
Like an apple tree among the trees of the wood.
In that shade I delight to sit
Tasting his sweet fruit. — Songs 2:3

The voice of my beloved: Here it comes!
Leaping over the mountains, skipping across the hills. — Songs 2:8

The voice of my beloved: Here it comes!
Leaping over the mountains, skipping across the hills.

My love is like a gazelle, a wild stag.
He stands there on the other side of our wall, gazing
Through the windows, peering through the lattice.

My Beloved speaks to me through every sound, taste,
fragrance, touch, color, light, emotion, and insight that
leaps into my consciousness… through the ordinary
miracles of each moment. My Lover knows no
obstacle to the pursuit of His Love. He leaps over the
mountains of my complacency, skips over the hills of
my disappointment, blinding doubt, numbing fear and
deeply ingrained habit.

I have built walls to keep You out. Such awesome love will
surely mean the destruction of my small world.

Yet in moments of great beauty, my thick and stubborn
opacity dissolves. I stand before You transparent,
trembling, at the intersection of my greatest terror and
my greatest longing—the place where I am finally seen.

My love is like a gazelle, a wild stag.
He stands there on the other side of our wall, gazing
Through the windows, peering through the lattice. —Songs 2:9

My beloved calls to me:

Arise my friend, oh beautiful one,
Go to yourself...

For now the winter is past,
The rains are over and gone,
Blossoms appear in the fields,
The time for singing has come.
The sound of the turtledove
Echoes throughout the land.

The fig tree is ripening
Its new green fruit,
And the budded vines give of their fragrance,
Arise my friend, oh beautiful one,
Go to yourself...

For now, my struggle is over. I struggled with the belief
that I shouldn't be exactly who I am and sing myself
aloud from the nearest tree. I struggled with the belief
that I should have a different fragrance—something
sweet or perhaps, something smarter, a fragrance that
might be acceptable, that might perhaps blend in. I
lost the battle against who I am, yet in my losing I am
victorious. In my losing I have found myself. My song
echoes throughout the land. I exult in the fragrance
that is mine alone.

My dove in the clefts of the rocks
Hidden by the cliff,
Let me see who you are,
Let me hear your voice,
Your sweet voice,
Your radiant face.

Yes, I have been hidden from my own eyes, and so hidden
    from You,
My only love. Hidden by shame in a crevice of the heart,
I bend to fit this dark cave.
My voice has been muffled, my light dimmed.
    My treasure—
    hidden away.

Catch us the foxes,
The little foxes that raid our vineyard
Just when the vines are in bloom.

I thought I heard my Beloved call to me... when suddenly
    hungry foxes are loosed in the mind! Those clever
    thoughts raid my vineyard just as the tender blossoms
    dare to make themselves known. "Who do you
    think you are?" the foxes rasp. One clever, cruel fox,
    disdaining the sweet blooms, points to the suffering
    in the world: war, disease, poverty, degradation... and
    then taunts, "How dare you celebrate? How dare you
    shine?"

My beloved is mine and I am his.
He pastures among the lilies.
Before the day blows on,
And the shadows flee,
Turn away, my love,
And be like a gazelle, a wild stag
On the jagged mountains.

Oh Mystery, You who dwell in the depths,
At the center of my every molecule,
At the heart of my being.

You glow beneath the brittle shallow surface of the world,
You burn inside the shadow.
You are shining through the dark with so much love…
'Til darkness itself shines.

We belong together—
You and I among the lilies.
I won't have you tamed, buttoned up inside priestly
    vestments,
Imprisoned in church, mosque or synagogue,
Turn away, my love, from definitions and dogma,
Turn away, from even my idea of You, my finite
    expectations,
Surprise me on the jagged mountain.

Blossoms appear in the fields,
The time for singing has come.
The sound of the turtledove
Echoes throughout the land. —Songs 2:12

3. Like a Pillar of Smoke

In my bed all night I long
For the one that my soul loves,
I seek him but do not find him.
I rise and roam the city,
Through the streets and through the squares
I search for the one that my soul loves,
I seek him everywhere but do not find him.

I seek him everywhere:
In the approval of my parents and teachers,
In achievement,
In the admiration of the young men,
In my compulsion to "figure it out,"
    in my thirst to unravel the mystery.
I seek him as I try to hold on to something, someone,
    anyone, anything that might assure me and reassure
    me of my worth. But I do not find him.

Then the watchmen who circle the city find me.
"Have you seen him? Have you seen the beloved of my
soul?"

I was lost in my longing, my looking, my lack, my
    desperation. And then the Light of Awareness found
    me, awakened me to the real question beneath all my
    grasping. Awareness freed me from the compulsion of
    the search, because I could suddenly see that although
    this was an arduous and dangerous journey—

I had already arrived.
The destination was beneath my feet.
The treasure was already safe within me.

Scarcely had they passed
when I found my soul's beloved,
I held him, I would not let him go
Until I brought him to my mother's house
Into the place where I had been conceived.

My Beloved, in the moment when you touch me,
I brim over with your sweetness,
I try to grasp it,
to save some for later,
share its abundance with my friends,
its bounty with the hungry world.

But it is impossible.

It would be like trying to grab smoke, to hold an ocean, or
to contain a fire that burns through every container.

When the Beloved comes, the only thing I can do is
consent.
I am lifted up by the smoke,
dissolved in the ocean,
transformed by the fire,

And in that moment of transformation I can know myself
before I was born, before I had a face to call "I".

Shefa Gold

Daughters of Jerusalem, swear to me
By the gazelles, by the deer in the field,
That you will not awaken love until it is ripe.

Oh sweet friends, trust the love that is awakened in me
    and then buried by the details of my life. Give me just
    one quiet moment of blessed stillness.

As the tumult settles I will hold in my hand
    the gift that I have been waiting to give.

Who is that rising from the wilderness,
Like a pillar of smoke,
Fragrant with myrrh and frankincense
From the powders of the merchant?

This wilderness is the place of transformation,
The place where I am purified for your love,
There I am made fragrant.

Only by journeying can we become lovers.
We will rise from the wilderness of alone-ness.
Together we will enter the Land of the Beloved,
    the place that flows with milk from the Great Mother
    and honey from the Rock—
Our Rock and Redeemer.

Here is Solomon's bed,
Surrounded by sixty warriors,
The heroes of Israel,
Each of them skilled in battle,
Each with a sword on his thigh
Against the terror of night.

On my Death-bed, I am reminded
    that I am well-guarded,
        and honored by all the love I have given.
The sword of Truth is brandished in protection
    of all I cherish,
It is wielded now against the terror of Night, against the
    terror of Not-Being.

King Solomon built a pavilion
From the cedars of Lebanon,
He made its columns of silver,
Its cushions of gold,
Its couches of purple linen,
And the daughters of Jerusalem
    inlaid it with love.
Oh daughters of Zion,
Come out and gaze upon King Solomon
    with the crown his mother gave him
    on his wedding day,
The day of his heart's rejoicing.

When I love, I build a palace. Relationships come and go through the ruin of divorce, the tragedy of Death, the misunderstandings that come with being human. Yet the palace of this love withstands every storm, every earth-quaking change. Each day that my heart rejoices in love, I inlay another precious stone on the steps of the palace. With each song I sing from this pure love, I weave another tapestry with my memories, dreams and desires.

Love is never wasted. Even when I feel rejected or suspect that my love is not received; even if no one hears my song, reads my words or appreciates the effort... Each moment is an opportunity to love my life and be loved by it, and in doing this I am building the Palace of my Soul.

Your hair is Like a flock of goats Streaming down Mount GILEAD. 4:1

Your hair
Like a flock of goats
Trailing down Mount Gilead. — *Songs 4:1*

Shefa Gold

4. This Moment of Love

How beautiful you are, my friend,
How beautiful!
Your eyes are doves behind the thicket of your hair,

Your hair
Like a flock of goats
Trailing down Mount Gilead.

Your teeth like a flock of ewes
That come up white from washing,
All of them alike, all shining and present.

Your lips like a scarlet ribbon
And your voice so sweet.

The curve of your cheek
Like a pomegranate
Hidden behind the thicket of your hair,

Your neck is a tower of David
Built to perfection,
A thousand shields hang upon it,
All the armor of heroes.

Your breasts are two fawns,
Twins of a gazelle,
Pasturing among the lilies.

My hair is thinning and going gray.
My breasts will never perch firm and high,
     pasturing on the lilies of my chest.
My nose will never be straight; my teeth are no longer
     white and shining. The tower of my neck seems to sag
     under the weight of each passing season, trampled
     beneath the relentless hooves of Time.
My once moist lips chap and dry in the desert sun.

And yet you know me as Beautiful, perfect,
     without blemish!

And You, my Beloved... this world you wear as a garment
     is torn and stained; ripped apart:
     by war;
     by greed;
     by despair;
     by rage.
Your magnificent garment decays in disease and injustice,
Its cloth is rotting in poverty and degradation.

And yet I know You truly in your incomparable beauty
     and perfection. Beneath that beggar's disguise, You are
     my Shining King, without blemish.

Before the day blows on
And the shadows flee,
I will go myself to the mountain of myrrh,
To the hill of frankincense.

You are all-beautiful, my friend,
There is no blemish in you.
Oh come with me my bride,
Come down from Lebanon
Down from the peaks of Amana
Down from Senir and Hermon,
From the mountains of the leopards,
The lion's den.

I am called down from the arrogant heights of my
    isolation, my illusions of separateness. I am called out
    from the lion's den, where I've been chewing on the
    same dry bone for eons… growling between naps.

You call me out of my cave, and I hear you say, with only a
    hint of exasperation, "Come down from your pretense!
    I don't care what you're wearing, how much money you
    have, how successful you seem.
I know who you really are.
    I know how beautiful you are my friend.
    You can come out of hiding now."

You have ravished my heart,
My sister, my bride,
You have ravished my heart
With one glance of your eyes,
With one bead of your necklace.

Infatuation may be blind, but this true love sees to the
    core of beauty… Ravishing the Heart of Reality,

destroying the mask that keeps us apart, that keeps us
separate. I am sister to all Life, bride to the Beloved.

How sweet is your loving,
My sister, my bride,
How much better than wine!
Your oils, more fragrant than any spice.

Your lips, my bride, drip honey,
Honey and milk are under your tongue,
And your clothes hold the scent of Lebanon.

Our Promised Land flows with milk and honey,
It can be conjured with a word,
Entered with a kiss.
A forty year journey from slavery to Freedom—
    is accomplished by us in this moment of Love.

An enclosed garden is my sister, my bride
A hidden fountain, a sealed spring.
Your watered fields are
. an orchard of pomegranate trees
    laden with delicious fruit,
    flowering henna and spikenard,
    spikenard and saffron, cane and cinnamon,
    with every tree of frankincense,
    myrrh and aloes,
    all the finest perfumes.

Shefa Gold

Sweetness drops from your lips O bride,
Honey and milk are under your tongue.
And the scent of your robes
is like the scent of Lebanon.
4:11

Your lips, my bride, drip honey,
Honey and milk are under your tongue,
And your clothes hold the scent of Lebanon.—Songs 4:11

עורי צפון ובואי תימן הפיחי גני יזלו בשמיו יבא דודי

לגנו ויאכל פרי מגדיו

Awake O North Wind, Come O south wind! Blow upon my garden that its perfume may spread. Let my beloved come to his garden And enjoy its lecious fRoits. 4:16

Awake North wind! Oh South wind, come!
Blow upon my garden
And let its spices stream out.
Let my lover come into his garden
And taste its luscious fruit. —Songs 4:16.

You are a garden spring,
A well of living waters
That flow from Lebanon.

I am hidden, even to myself.
The secret is revealed in the unselfconscious flow
    of my love.
Only You, my Beloved Mysterious Infinite Void, can call
    forth and receive this infinite flow... through the vessel
    that I am becoming.
With this stream of love,
    You make me known to myself.

Awake North wind! Oh South wind, come!
Blow upon my garden
And let its spices stream out.
Let my lover come into his garden
And taste its luscious fruit.

I invite the winds of change to blow into my life.
Who can fortify against them?
I do not resist,
I welcome them, honor them;
They whip through me—
I vow to ride the winds, to consciously use their force to
    free myself,
To liberate my true fragrance—
    so that I might bless the world with my unique essence.

I vow to receive Life in both its awesomeness and its
    awfulness, all of it.

My garden is dynamic,
  ever-changing,
   ever-seeding,
    ever-sprouting,
     ever-greening,
      ever-blossoming,
       ever-fruiting,
        ever-rotting,
         ever-going-back-to-seed.
I offer these seeds to the winds.

Catch them, carry them, take them!
"You never know!"

You never know what seeds will take root, somewhere
   in someone. You never know what will grow, how or
   when.

Within my garden that is buzzing with life and change,
   disaster and renewal, storm and bright sun, fragility
   and resilience… there is a center of calm, my still and
   spacious, waiting, open heart.

Into that center I invite the Beloved.

5. In The Fever of Love

I have come into my garden,
My sister, my bride,
I have gathered my myrrh and my spices,
I have eaten from my honeycomb,
I have drunk my wine and my milk.

You enter this garden, breach my defenses,
   break open the gates to the innermost recesses of my soul,
That I might know Your sweetness, taste Your nectar.
Those spices that I thought were my own true essence
Are gathered up by my Beloved to become part of the
   Divine Body.
I surrender the wine of my intoxication
   and the milk of all that I have to give,
I am consumed by that Great Mystery.

In surrendering all that I am to His pleasure, I come to
   know myself, my goodness, beauty and uniqueness
   as if for the first time.
When You feast in this garden of my life,
I am honored to suckle the whole of creation with
   my milk. The wine of my inspiration will gladden the
   cosmos.

When I sing these words to You,
   I exult in the richness of this life.
I fully inhabit this world, this body,
   this particular circumstance.

I celebrate the consummation of our Love.
Not only have I yearned to enter Eden; I have arrived!
I drink in the pleasure of being human.
I drink to my Beloved.

Feast, friends, and drink till you are drunk with love!

Yes, this is how to live life! Each day a feast of taste, color
and experience is set before me. I am commanded to
know life intimately, to experience the whole range of
what it means to be human, to quench my thirst for
knowledge and pleasure.

This drunkenness is the roar of ocean
beyond the shore of words,
I let the taste of finite things send me
beyond the things themselves
to the Infinite mystery that beckons me.
I share this feast with everyone and anyone who has made
not only a commitment to love,
but a commitment to celebrate love.

I was asleep but my heart stayed awake.
There it is… the sound of my lover knocking:

I am asleep,
lulled by the news and the constant din
of media and commerce.
I am in a trance,
I collude with agreed-upon reality.
I am trapped,

I am stranded on the dry surface of my life,
    while an underground river flows beneath me
    unseen and untouched.

Yet there is a place in my heart that has stayed awake
    and is constantly awakening through the power of its
    yearning, through the pulse of its desire. The eyes of
    my heart blink open and the ears of my heart remain
    vigilant, attentive to the call of Love. The sound is
    elusive yet persistent in its effort to break through the
    din of confusion and busyness that surrounds and fills
    my daily routines.

The sound of my lover knocking—the momentary startle
    of finding myself *so* alive and vulnerable and touched
    by a color, a tender breeze, a word whispered to me in
    the darkness, a vivid memory or a sudden knowing.

With my heart awake I hear the call to Love
    which is the call to glowing and lucid aliveness.

Open to me, my sister, my friend,
My dove, my perfect one!
My head is wet with dew,
My hair drenched in the damp of night.

In that state of aliveness, I hear the call of Love,
God-as-Love entices me with His sweetness
    and reminds me that I must let Him in.
In my forgetfulness and distraction,
I have closed the door.

Everything depends on the simple gesture
　of opening,
　　of turning,
　　　of letting God in.

Every relationship depends on my ability to open, to
　　hear the real question that is left unspoken. When I
　　am open, I can know and respond to the desires of my
　　beloved whose desire may be hidden even from himself.

I knock.
I call out to the world, with all my sweet longing,
　"Open to me…
Let there be a space for what I yearn to give,
Let me find the door to fulfillment,
　adventure, comfort, enlightenment, honor.
World, I call on you as my friend,
　my kin,
　　my ally,
Lover, let me in."

Shefa Gold

But I have taken off my robes,
How can I dress again?
I have bathed my feet,
Must I dirty them?

When Love calls it is almost always at an inconvenient
time. All the plans I have made must be scrapped
and my heart must be torn open. This hesitation in
answering the door is born of my complacency, my
addictions, my dependence on the known and
predictable. Deep down I know that when that door
opens, everything in my life may have to change. All
my careful planning, all my clever manipulations will
be for nothing. My well-built illusion of control will be
shattered. Complacency has shrouded my awareness
and for a moment I am numb to the urgency of this
"Now." My heart closes in habit. My ears are deaf to
the sound of my Beloved. I just want to go back to
sleep. When I miss the opportunity for Love, it is a
moment of tragic betrayal.

My love reached in for the latch
And deep within me, my heart stirred.

Even through this numbness, this complacency,
My heart has stayed awake.
Its longing finally stirs me.
The beat of my yearning heart rouses me
    from my paralysis.
My stubborn habits and inertia have almost prevented
    my heart's desire— the meeting of Love.

In my hesitation, I may have missed my chance for Love.

I am like the Israelites who have been told they must
    leave Egypt immediately when Freedom calls. There
    is not even time to let the bread rise. I have been more
    concerned with my bread than my freedom.

I rose to open to my love
My hands dripping myrrh
My fingers flowing myrrh
On the doorbolt.

I must rise, to open.
I rise from my couch.
I rise above my petty concerns,
I take the wide perspective and lift myself up
    above all entanglements,
Only then can I open to Love.
My hands "dripping myrrh" are a sure sign
    that dry hesitation has been transformed
    into the passion
    that is necessary for me to finally act.

I opened to my love,
But he had turned away and was gone.
My soul fled when he spoke.

No longer numb,
I feel the full pain of separation from Love,
It is as if my own soul has left me.

Shefa Gold

I looked for him, but could not find him,
I called, but he did not answer,

The power of my yearning revives me,
Though I do not find my Beloved, I begin to find my
   own voice, my own Passion. The silence that answers
   my call inspires me to call with more sweetness, more
   vitality.

Then the watchmen who circle the city
Found me,
They beat me, they bruised me
The watchmen of the walls
Tore the shawl from my shoulders.

The story of awakening: I was so much more comfortable
   asleep. The "watchmen," Awareness itself, will not
   allow the old self and its layers of defense to survive.
   They tear the shawl from my shoulder, stripping away
   my disguise, leaving me vulnerable to the pain of
   loving.

If I protect myself from that Pain,
   The Joy of Love will also be withheld.

Old habits lure me back to sleep, murmuring that I will
   be beaten and bruised by Life's constant changes. But
   only Awake can I finally meet Love and become Your
   powerful and passionate Divine partner.

Swear to me, daughters of Jerusalem
If you find my beloved,
You must tell him
That I am in the fever of Love.

I call on my sisters, my friends, my spirit-buddies to
    witness my dilemma and hold me true
    to my deepest wishes, my highest dreams.

You help me to search my own heart,
And provide a mirror for my predicament.
Your questions help me to refine
    my deepest intention for love,
You challenge me to live from my integrity,
To dance the path of my Song.

How is your lover unique,
Oh most beautiful of women?
How is your lover unique
That we must swear to you?

My sisters call to me,
They call me to share the beauty that is hidden,
They ask me to turn myself inside out
    in the name of Love,
They challenge me to speak the un-nameable,
    to create vessels that might hold oceans.

The daughters of Jerusalem dare me to BE the Beloved,
    to be fully myself.

                    Shefa Gold

My beloved is radiant and earthy
He towers above ten thousand.
His head is burnished gold,
The wave of his hair
Shiny black as the raven,

His eyes like doves
By the flowing rivers
    of milk and plenty.
His cheeks are a bed of spices,
Treasures of sweet perfume,
His lips red lilies
Wet with myrrh.

His hands are rods of gold,
Studded with topaz,
His body is polished ivory,
Inlaid with sapphire,
His thighs are marble pillars
On pedestals of gold.
Majestic as Lebanon,
A man like a cedar!

His mouth is luscious,
He is all delight.

His head is finest gold.
His Locks are curled
And black as a RAVEN.
5:11

His head is burnished gold,
The wave of his hair
Shiny black as the raven. —Songs 5:11

How shall I embrace this life that I have been given?

I begin with my breath.
Breathing fully and deeply, I take in the treasures of sweet
   perfume. I feel the earth beneath my feet, supporting
   me with its wide embrace. I open my eyes to color—
   rich hues of sapphire-blue, verdant shades of gracious
   greens, red lilies that celebrate themselves, gesturing
   seductively. I open my ears to the music of flowing
   rivers, to the flutter of wings, to the symphony of winds
   rushing through cedar.

I open my senses to subtle textures
      that speak so articulately,
      to the spice that awakens the heart of memory.

This is my beloved
And this is my friend,
Oh daughters of Jerusalem.

Who is that rising like the morning star?
Clear as the moon, bright as the sun,
Daunting as the stars in the sky. —Song 6:10

6. Leaning Into Love's Embrace

Where has your lover gone,
Oh most beautiful of women?
Where has your beloved turned?
Tell us and we will seek him with you.

On the Path of Love I seek out friends who will ask me
the right questions; who will find me when I am lost;
who will remind me when I forget. I dedicate the
fruits of my practice to these companions. I give them
permission to rebuke me when I betray myself; to help
me laugh at myself when I am lost in tragedy; to help
me see the big picture when I am mired in minutiae;
to remind me of the startling details when I become
intoxicated with the cosmos.

My love has gone down to his garden,
To the beds of spices,
To graze and to gather lilies.

I am my beloved's and my beloved is mine,
He pastures among the lilies.

In seeking the Beloved, I must sometimes go outside my
ideas, my learning, my civilized conventions. I don't
have to go far.

That garden of spices is just past my door.

But my window is double-paned, weatherproof, wind-
resistant glass, with a screen to keep the bugs out. And
my door is locked against intruders, secured against
the elements.

Yes, I am my Beloved's and my Beloved is mine.
I must risk *everything* to be with You.

My friend, you are as beautiful as Tirzah,
Majestic as Jerusalem,
Daunting as the stars in the sky.

Turn your eyes away,
For they dazzle me.

Your hair
Like a flock of goats
Trailing down Mount Gilead.

Your teeth like a flock of ewes
That come up white from washing,
All of them alike, all shining and present.

The curve of your cheek
Like a pomegranate
Hidden behind the thicket of your hair,

I didn't quite believe you before,
    so you tell me again and again.
Every day as the sun comes up over the mesa,
You shine my own true beauty back to me.

When I can receive that true light,
My Beloved and I become mirrors for each other,
   reflecting endlessly...
Then the Light that was hidden away before Creation,
Shines out through my eyes.

There are sixty queens,
And eighty concubines,
And young maidens beyond number.

One alone is my dove, my perfect one,
One alone so luminous in her mother's heart.

The little girl inside asks, "Who, me?"

"Is my heart wide enough to receive the Great Love? Am
   I worthy? Will I dissolve under that Divine gaze? Will
   I shatter under the weight of your faith in me? Will I
   disappoint You?"

The Great Mother
Who is birthing Creation in every moment
   knows me,
She knows my unique light,
She sends me to walk this Path of Love.

Every maiden delights in her,
Queens and concubines praise her:

"Who is that rising like the morning star?
Clear as the moon, bright as the sun,
Daunting as the stars in the sky."

100 billion galaxies.
I try to understand. I try to fathom
   the wisdom of cosmologists.
We live in a tiny corner of one galaxy,
In a small cul-de-sac called the Milky Way.
This is my daily practice:
I say to myself, "There are 100 billion galaxies!"
I try to fathom; I am daunted.
My mind, just a tiny corner of a galaxy,
   is not big enough to hold this, but I try…
   and then my mind just shuts down.
I take a breath,
I close my eyes,
I fall into my heart…
   which is LARGER than 100 billion galaxies.
There, I rest,
   expanding out towards the edges of the universe,
   leaning into Love's embrace.

I went down to the nut grove,
To see the new green by the brook,
To see if the vines had blossomed
And the pomegranates had bloomed,

And oh, before I knew it,
She sat me down in the most noble of chariots.

And oh, before I knew it,
She sat me down in the most noble of chariots. —Songs 6:12

The chariot moves between worlds.
It is the vehicle that connects
the finite with the infinite,
Earth and Heaven,
Human and Divine.

The chariot holds the mystery
to the consummation of the Great Love.

7. There I will Give You My Love

Turn and return, Oh Shulamit,
Turn and return that we may gaze upon you!

Why do you gaze upon the Shulamit
As she dances through the camp?

I am riveted to her beauty. She is pure color, essence of
fragrance, true vitality, hidden grace. She reaches out a
delicate hand of invitation that I might join her in this
dance of turning.

And this is my dance:

Turning
   away from the habits of shallow breathing,
Returning
   to my true depths,
Turning
   away from cynical judgments—
   my armor against the terror of being judged in turn,
Returning
   to my open heart,
   where the courage and humility to remain vulnerable
   yield treasure upon treasure of surprises.

This is my dance:
Remembering,
   Forgetting,
      and Remembering again.

How graceful your steps in those sandals,
Oh nobleman's daughter.

The curves of your thigh are like jewels
Shaped by a master craftsmen,

Your navel is the moon's goblet,
Ever filled with wine,

Your belly is a mound of wheat,
Fringed with lilies,
Your breasts are two fawns,
Twins of a gazelle.

Your neck is a tower of ivory,
Your eyes are pools in Heshbon,
By the gates of Bat-Rabbim,

Your nose, like a tower of Lebanon
That turns towards Damascus,

Your head crowns you like Mount Carmel,
And the hair of your head is like royal purple,
A king is held captive in its tresses.

Shefa Gold

Let us go early to the vineyards
To see if the vine has budded
If the blossoms have opened
And the pomegranates are in bloom. —Songs 7:13

In the Fever of Love

How beautiful and how sweet is Love
In all its pleasures!

How demanding and how rigorous is Love
In all its requirements!

Love asks Everything of me,

Scouring my heart for whatever I might be withholding;
She calls me into power and commands my full attention,
She crowns me with my own royal purple potential,
Her music shapes this dance with meticulous grace.

If I listen well, get out of my own way, give honor to this
    curve of thigh, this mound of belly... then I will be
    danced. I will be held in Love's embrace.
As my heart expands, I am called each day to receive this
    gift of Life from You, my Beloved; I am called to pour
    myself out in response to Your flow. You flow through
    my body...

Here is the challenge I face:
Unless I give myself to You—my flesh becomes stiff,
    numb, inert, un-responsive and closed...

Your Great Love pours through this world
    Through muscle, bone, sinew and fat.
Your Great Love is written
    in the smiling wrinkles of my face
    just as my Life is engraved on the palm of Your Hand.
This Love calls me to embodiment.

Your stature seemed tall as a palm tree,
And your breasts, the clusters of its fruit.

I said, "Let me climb into that palm tree,
And take hold of its branches."

May your breasts be like clusters
Of grapes on a vine,

The fragrance of your breath

Like apples,
And your mouth, like the best wine.

I climb into the Tree of Life,
I take hold of its branches,
I climb into my own skin,
    inhabiting this body,
My breath
    is the sweetest fruit.
Its fragrance is the gift that I give in each moment,
    my only true gift.

Let it flow smoothly to my beloved,
Gliding between sleepy lips,

I am my beloved's
And his longing is for me,
Only for me.

Come, my beloved,
Let us go out to the field
And lie all night among the flowering henna,

Let us go early to the vineyards
To see if the vine has budded,
If the blossoms have opened,
And the pomegranates are in bloom,

There I will give you my love.

The mandrakes yield their fragrance
And at our doors are all kinds of precious fruits,
Both newly picked and long-stored,
I have hidden them away for you.

I am given as a gift to this life,
My small life is a gift to the whole,
The cosmos longs to know itself through me!
I hear this longing in the call to adventure,
    the call to journey within and beyond.

Come, my beloved, Let us go out to the field.
Come my beloved, let us leave the comfort of familiar
    habit; let us challenge these walls, fling open these
    doors; explode definition; shatter this outgrown
    identity. Let us dare to disagree with the wardens of
    Time and Space; let us step outside possibility.

There I will give you my love.

Come my beloved, let us go down into the valley, to see
  if the cottonwood has budded its new green, to caress
  the feather of mountain mahogany, and breathe in the
  butterscotch of pine-sap flowing. My precious fruits,
  both newly picked and long-stored, have been hidden
  away too long. Whatever I don't give away will decay
  and fester and become misery.

Let us go out to the field...

Where spaciousness can untie my tangles,
Where tantalizing fragrance can inspire my curiosity,
Where I can lose my apprehension, find my humor,
Play in the soil of the Ancestors,
  bury treasures for my descendants,
And open to my true desire.

There I will give you my love.

philipratner 7:16

I would bring you to my mother's house,
And she would teach me,
I would give you spiced wine to drink. —Songs 8:2

Shefa Gold

8. Let Me Enter Your Garden

Oh that you were my brother,
And had nursed at my mother's breast!
I would kiss you in the streets
And no one would scorn me.

Oh that my intimacy with You could be completely
   revealed! This wild passionate love that is my source
   of vitality, humor, pleasure and wisdom… has become
   hidden, nearly shameful. I sneak a kiss and then turn
   back to my computer. I laugh secretly and then put on
   a straight face.

I would bring you to my mother's house,
And she would teach me,
I would give you spiced wine to drink,
My pomegranate wine.

I would stand before the Great Mother who is birthing
   this world in every moment and she would teach me to
   open.
She would teach me to release sadness,
   spread joy,
      focus anger
         and clear the ashes on the altar of my heart.
I would finally share
   that superbly aged and ripened wine—
   my passion that has been hidden away.

I have been waiting my whole life for the right occasion.
That time is now. And now. And now.

His left hand beneath my head,
His right arm embracing me,

I lean into your warm embrace.
I release a lifetime of tension, doubt, control,
I have been holding on so tightly and now I let go
    so that I can know that I am held.

Daughters of Jerusalem, swear to me
That you will not awaken love
Until it is ripe.

Friends of my soul, will you touch the soft of my skin,
    taste the pulp of my sweetness, inquire with curiosity
    till you know the seed hidden within? Will you mirror
    back to me my true taste in this ripened moment of
    celebration?

Who is that rising from the wilderness
Leaning upon her beloved?

Who is that peering through the lattice, opening the gate
    that I thought was locked, entering in to my garden,
    bending down to so tenderly touch the petal and
    breathe in the fragrance at my core?

Shefa Gold

His left hand beneath my head,
His right arm embracing me. —Songs 8:3

In the Fever of Love   75

Set me as a seal upon your heart,
A sign upon your arm,
For Love is as strong as Death. —Songs 8:6

In your Presence, all the hardness in me softens. As you
   lean against me, we both fall endlessly, past doubt,
   blame, shame, past all my excuses… into the expanded
   embrace of this miraculous Now.

I awakened you beneath the apple tree,
In that same place where your mother
Conceived and gave you life.

I dreamt of deception—just one simple slant on the truth
   leads me ever away from my Self, as I weave the ever-
   so-complicated web, and eventually the fortress to
   defend my "innocence."

You awakened me from this dream—You awakened
   me to the truth of my innocence which requires no
   defense. My purity contains the diamond-sharp
   shining power of Creation itself.

Set me as a seal upon your heart,
A sign upon your arm,
For Love is as strong as Death,
Its passion is as harsh as the grave,
Its sparks become a raging fire,
A Divine Flame.

Great seas cannot extinguish love
No river can wash it away,

If a man tried to buy Love
With all the wealth of his house,
He would only be scorned.

Yes, I have tried to buy Love,
   with my wit, my charm,
   with my know-how and elbow grease,
   with my determination, ambition, agility,
   beauty and humor.
And yes, I have been scorned—
   Not because I am undeserving of Love,
   But because the Love I seek is already mine.

The Divine Flame dances on,
   just below the surface of Tragedy,
That raging fire throwing out tiny sparks of Wisdom
Is the vast truth of Me.

Yet Tragedy pulls me with her drama. Death lures me,
   enticing my vulnerable shadow with a fascinating story.

Here is what saves me:
I close my eyes
And breathe into my own waiting heart.
The spark becomes a flame,
The flame becomes Light,
The Light becomes a gentle Radiance that reaches out
   to hold my whole world
      in her loving embrace.

Here is what saves me:
I know in my bones that
Through the devastation of loss,
The scope of my Love is revealed.
My Love is the hidden treasure that longs to be known.

We have a young sister
And she has no breasts,

What shall we do for our sister,
When she is courted?

If she is a wall, we will build
A silver turret upon her,
If she is a door, we will bolt her
With beams of cedar.

I am a wall
And my breasts are towers,
But for my lover, I will be
A city of Peace.

I feel the stirring of that place of vulnerability in me—
The soft of my heart that I have been protecting so loyally.

Finally she speaks, or finally I listen.

"I only seem small to you because you do not yet know or
trust me. All your protections, all your defenses have
shut me in. The courtship that you are delaying for me
(with your narrow fear) is the precious intimacy with the
Beloved who has been calling.
Don't you see?
It is the very reason you are here!"

Solomon had a vineyard in Baal-Hamon,
He gave that vineyard to watchmen,

Anyone would give a thousand pieces of silver
  for its fruit.

I have my very own vineyard,
So keep your thousands, Solomon,
And pay two hundred to those
Who must guard your fruit.

I have my very own vineyard.
Its precious fruit is unique, incomparable.
I have been searching the world for grapes like this,
Trespassing in the vineyards of Solomon,
While my own precious fruit
    has been sweetening on the vine,
    nurtured in the soil of this surprising life.
And all those rainstorms I have suffered
Have made my fruit plump with Compassion,
juicy with a love that is at once given and received.

Oh woman in the garden,
All our friends listen for your voice,
Let me hear it now!

Oh Woman in the garden,
    Oh Shechina,
    Ancient Mother,
    Origin hidden in all things!

Oh Holy Innerness shining out!
I listen for your voice…
    In the scent of gardenia

Shefa Gold

In the cry of a newborn,
In the silence before words are even possible.

Your face shines with a Light from Beyond.
You are crowned by my longing for You.
Let me open to Your Mystery,
Let me enter Your garden.

Hurry, my beloved,
Be my gazelle, my young stag
On the mountain of spices.

Shefa Gold

The Commandments
of the Song of Songs

Rabbi Akiva taught, "Had the Torah not been given, we could live our lives by the Song of Songs."[*]

For years I have immersed myself in this holy text - learning its language, receiving its passion, and entering into the reality it describes: the giving and receiving of Love. Though the Song of Songs describes a very human relationship, it is understood to illuminate all relationship, most importantly the relationship with God, that Mystery that shines forth from within and beyond this world. When Love flows freely between us and that Great Mystery, the whole world is watered and nourished.

I have lived with the question, "What would it mean to live my life by the Song of Songs?" Listening for its instruction, opening to its wisdom, I allow myself to be commanded by its voice.

---

[*]Shir HaShirim Zuta (Buber), cited in AJ Heschel's *Heavenly Torah* p. 196.

The Ten Commandments

1. Thou shalt explore intimacy, allowing thyself to be drawn by Mystery and be open to the power of yearning for God.

2. Thou shalt be fully engaged, enjoying what is before thee now, and learn to perceive the perfection beneath it, and behind this seemingly imperfect world.

3. Thou shalt cultivate generosity in appreciation of the beauty that is before thee.

4. Thou shalt truly experience pleasure and surrender to the intoxication of Love, occasionally losing "control."

5. Thou shalt experience and know thy complete purity and innocence and yet pay seasoned and careful attention to the timing of Love.

Shefa Gold

of the Song of Songs

6. Thou shalt be in conversation with Nature and through that conversation explore the Mystery of Love and Death.

7. Thou shalt treasure, protect and honor the gifts given to thee and allow thyself to be addressed personally by God through the gifts of this world.

8. Thou shalt invite all the winds of the world to blow upon thee and receive each gust of change as a summons to strengthen your commitment to fully waking up.

9. Thou shalt discern the uniqueness in each opportunity for love and risk everything in order to rise to the challenge of Love

10. Thou shalt play... with enthusiasm and curiosity while listening attentively for the voice of the Shechinah.

1. Thou shalt explore intimacy,
allowing thyself to be drawn by Mystery
and be open to the power of yearning for God.

Oh, give me the kisses of your mouth,
For your sweet loving is better than wine....
The very first words of Song of Songs send us on the journey of relationship. We don't ask to hold hands or turn our face for a peck on the cheek. We are commanded to pucker up; to meet the fullness of Life and Love, to explore the boundaries of our separate self, and to keep challenging those boundaries. Every word of Song of Songs can be read as both the word that I speak to God and the word that God speaks to me. As we ask for Love, we must also rise to its challenge.

Each relationship in our lives opens the door to a whole new universe. This relationship can be with a beloved other, with a parent, friend, or with the world around us. Glimpsing ourselves through the eyes of this "other" allows us to escape from the confining prison of self. Once free, and yet connected, we are drawn by the Mystery of innumerable galaxies, swirling around each other, also interconnected.

As we stand in awe of this vast cosmic drama, we experience it all unfolding within a great Oneness, the Unity that embraces us all. That great *Echad* is supremely conscious and supremely loving.

In a moment of loving we can feel ourselves inside that Oneness. This moment is fleeting, but once it is gone, it is replaced with a new feeling: Yearning. Once we have tasted of this Oneness, we long for more and the power of Yearning is unlocked. This is the power that inspires us to free ourselves from separateness and propels us into the arms of the Beloved.

Shefa Gold

2. Thou shalt be fully engaged,
enjoying what is before thee now,
and learn to perceive the perfection beneath and
behind this seemingly imperfect world.

The challenge of Love requires that we not hold anything
in reserve. We are commanded to be fully engaged with
Life. When we experience fully our present moment, we
fulfill the injunction to "Love God with all your heart and
all your soul and all your might."

I have been on various Buddhist-style retreats where
I received instruction to pay attention to my breath.
The instruction was helpful at the time. Later, I had the
wonderful experience of hearing Thich Nat Han teach this
same practice in a new way. In the most sensuous tone of
voice he said, "Enjoy your breathing!" That changed the
practice for me. In order to really "enjoy," I also needed to
pay attention, but it brought me a step further. I found I
could open to the gift of each breath, and receive its bounty.
The Song commands us to bask in the miracle of whatever
we find before us:

Wherever we lie, our bed is green,
Our roofbeams are cedar, our rafters, fir.

When the lovers of the Song of Songs see each other as
"perfect," it may seem that they have been blinded by Love.
On the contrary, their eyes have been opened to a deeper
perfection previously obscured by the outer surface. Our
whole world wears a mask of Tragedy. The perception of
"everything that is wrong" is so compelling, that it takes the
most powerful force in the universe to pry that mask loose—
even for a moment—so that we can receive the perfection
that underlies all of Reality. We return from that experience
of perfection with a challenge to expand our consciousness
ever wider to embrace this paradox, to see the perfection
which lies beneath the imperfection.

3. Thou shalt cultivate generosity
in appreciation of the beauty
that is before thee.

The Language of Song of Songs teaches us to be extravagant with praise. The Lovers of the Song make a gift of their expressive, warm attention, always finding new gifts of admiration to shower upon each other. The Song commands us to cultivate that same generosity of spirit: We are invited to look for the good in others and to extend our capacity for giving.

You are all-beautiful, my friend,
There is no blemish in you.

There are so many teachings in our Tradition about *Lashon HaRa* ("bad speech"), rules limiting harmful talk, because words are such a powerful force for us. The Song turns this teaching around by commanding us instead to express the *goodness* that rests in our hearts. If you have something nice to say and you *don't* say it, you have broken a commandment of the Song.

To praise is a transformative act: It changes the giver and the recipient, both. Expressing our appreciation for beauty lifts us up to the level of the object of our praise. To be in relationship in this deeply affirming way unlocks the power to raise both Self and Other to a higher level.

4. Thou shalt truly experience pleasure
and surrender to the intoxication of Love,
occasionally losing "control."

He brought me to the tavern,
And His banner over me is Love.

The "tavern" of mystical literature is the place we go to be freed from categories, definitions and concepts regarding the nature of Self, God or Reality. There we can be "claimed" by the naked truth of our direct experience—unmediated by our notions about what is desirable, or real, or even possible. We are commanded to relinquish control... (which is to actually abandon the illusion of control) long enough to be filled to overflowing with a Spirit that cannot be tamed or contained. The Song of Songs commands us:

Feast, friends, and drink
till you are drunk with love!

5. Thou shalt experience and know thy complete purity and innocence
and yet pay seasoned and careful attention to the timing of Love.

The Song of Songs commands us to be Lovers and to know our love as something completely innocent and pure. Love requires nothing in return. Love leaves little room for shame, fear, or ulterior motives. In the heart of hearts lies the sweet radiance of our true self underneath all the layers of false self. We are commanded to allow that radiance to shine forth into the world. Although this shining Love is completely innocent, through Life's lessons we must acquire the wisdom that Love holds in store for us. These words of warning are repeated three times:

Daughters of Jerusalem, swear to me,
By the gazelles, by the deer in the field,
that you will not awaken love
until it is ripe.

As the powerful forces of Love move through us, we bring all of our wisdom and sensitivity to bear. Timing is crucial. The right word spoken at the wrong time can destroy Life rather than create it. We must open ourselves to discerning the rhythms and tides of Love: knowing when to act, when to speak, when to remain silent, and how to wait for the Beloved.

6. Thou shalt be in conversation with Nature
and through that conversation explore the Mystery of Love and Death.

God speaks to us through the wonders and beauty and mysteries of Nature: We must learn how to listen. We are commanded to go out:

To see the new green by the brook,
To see if the vines had blossomed
And the pomegranates had bloomed.

Not only must we listen and watch and wonder, but we must know our own wildness, experience all the passion of being a holy animal. We are commanded to:

Be like a gazelle, a wild stag
On the jagged mountains.

As we get to know the cycles and rhythms of the Natural world and begin living the rhythms of moon and tide, seed and harvest—the power and intimacy of Love can transform us. Our conversation with Nature deepens, and we begin to notice that in every death, the seeds of new birth are hidden. With the Lovers in the Song of Songs we cry:

For Love is as strong as Death
Its passion is as harsh as the grave,
Its sparks become a raging fire,
A Divine Flame.

7. Thou shalt treasure, protect and honor the gifts given to thee

and allow thyself to be addressed personally by God through the gifts of this world.

We are commanded to open our eyes and enliven all of our senses so that we can appreciate the garden of our lives as exceedingly precious. Each fragrance, each color, each touch, each moment represents the fruit of eternity.

The Song of Songs commands us to treasure each day, to hold sacred each opportunity for the giving and receiving of Love.

> *My beloved calls to me:*
> *Arise my friend, oh beautiful one,*
> *Go to yourself…*
> *For now the winter is past,*
> *The rains are over and gone,*
> *Blossoms appear in the fields,*
> *The time for singing has come.*

When we awaken to this preciousness of our lives, we can begin living (and singing) from this awareness.

We must call on every ounce of strength and integrity in us to protect what we love and to never take it for granted. We are commanded to honor the gift of new life as it is re-created in us at every moment. The Song commands us to receive and open the personal letter that God has written to us—encoded in the details of our everyday life.

8. Thou shalt invite all the winds of the world to blow upon thee

and receive each gust of change as a summons to strengthen your commitment to fully waking up.

So much of our energy is habitually directed towards protecting ourselves from the winds of change. We hunker down and hope to stay hidden from tumult and the ravages of Time. In our attempt to hide our flaws, we allow our treasures to lie buried, concealed even from ourselves. The Song of Songs commands us to invite into our lives the transformative force of change. Change carries insight, possibility, and new perspectives. Only then can our fragrance, the uniqueness of who we are and are becoming, be revealed.

> *Awake North wind! Oh South wind, come!*
> *Blow upon my garden*
> *and let its spices stream out.*
> *Let my lover come into his garden*
> *And taste its luscious fruit.*

We are commanded to open to the energy of each direction of the compass, to invite each aspect of awakening to blow through the garden of our souls. We invite the winds of change to awaken our unique essence so that our treasures can be released by the gusts and shared.

9. Thou shalt discern the uniqueness in each opportunity for love
and risk everything in order to rise to the challenge of Love.

I am my beloved's
And his longing is for me,
Only for me.

When I live my life by the Song of Songs, I can't just say, "Oh I love everyone or everything...." Each person, color, flower, river, place has an essence that's waiting to be discovered by my attention and love. Although there is a great web of inter-connectedness that draws us together in its weave, each being stands in its uniqueness. I must stand in my own uniqueness in order to discover and appreciate the uniqueness of another. To experience my own uniqueness means to embark upon a path of self-knowledge and self-realization.

There are sixty queens,
And eighty concubines,
And young maidens beyond number.
One alone is my dove, my perfect one,
One alone so luminous in her mother's heart.

10. Thou shalt play...
with enthusiasm and curiosity
while listening attentively
for the voice of the Shechinah.

Playing helps us to find our power, our humor, and our love. We are commanded to "Go out and play!" Experiment with who you think you are. Try on some new identities. The Song commands us to be a wild stag, a King, a shepherd, or a mare among Pharaoh's chariots. In other words... it is an invitation to Play! Without playing, we become grim and dull. The Song commands us not to take ourselves so seriously. It would be better to take our playing more seriously!

Imagination is essential. Without a dynamic and fluid vision of Love, we cannot attempt to rise to Love's heights or explore its depths. Imagination expands the range of what we consider *possible*. We cultivate the imagination by taking time to dream; closing our eyes to outer distractions, we open the eye of the heart to inner treasures. We nurture the imagination by honoring the images, feelings, colors and flavors that are glimpsed, and by planting those glimpses as seeds in the fertile soil of our lives. We refine the imagination through continual and concerted practice.

Oh woman in the garden,
All our friends listen for your voice,
Let me hear it now!

Our passion, creativity, playfulness and imagination allow us to enter the Garden. And there, the Song tells us, we must listen for Her voice, that Divine voice that has been whispering to us all along.

About the Author

Rabbi Shefa Gold is a leader in Aleph: the Alliance for Jewish Renewal and received her ordination both from the Reconstructionist Rabbinical College and from Rabbi Zalman Schachter-Shalomi. She is the director of C-DEEP, The Center for Devotional Energy and Ecstatic Practice in Jemez Springs, New Mexico. Shefa composes and performs spiritual music, and has produced ten albums. One of those CDs, "Shir Delight: A Journey through the Song of Songs," is an excellent companion to this book.

Rabbi Gold teaches workshops and leads retreats on Chant, Devotional Healing, Spiritual Community Building, and Meditation. With her husband, Rachmiel O'Regan, she conducts workshops for couples based on the values articulated in The Song of Songs.

They train Chant Leaders in Kol Zimra, a two year program for rabbis, cantors and lay leaders. Rabbi Gold is also on the faculty of the Institute for Jewish Spirituality. Shefa combines her grounding in Judaism with a background in Buddhist, Christian, Islamic, and Native American spiritual traditions to make her uniquely qualified as a spiritual bridge celebrating the shared path of devotion. She is the author of *Torah Journeys: The Inner Path to the Promised Land*, also published by Ben Yehuda Press.

For information about how to order CD's and about Shefa's teaching schedule, visit her website: www.RabbiShefaGold.com

A Note on the Art
Phillip Ratner on the Song of Songs

Falling in love at first sight is exactly what happened with me and the Bible. Starting Hebrew School at about nine years old, I was mesmerized by every figure and adventure in this astonishing Book. It could never have occurred to me then or even later that I could make a life's work out of a volume five thousand years old. After more than twenty years of teaching, and of building my reputation as an artist with the eventual project of creating more than forty pieces of sculpture for permanent placement at Ellis Island and five bronzes standing permanently at the base of the Statue of Liberty, I was ready to pursue my life's dream.

The stories of Genesis and Exodus continued to intoxicate my imagination and eventually culminated in the establishment of two museums, one in Israel and one in America, on the theme of the Bible. The museums are the Israel Bible Museum in Safed, Israel, and the Dennis & Phillip Ratner Museum in suburban Washington, D.C.

It was not until my forties that I began to understand and appreciate what Judaism calls "The Writings." Ecclesiastes, Psalms, Job, and the Song of Songs demand more life experience for a true appreciation of them. Each of these has been source material for my work. It took another stage of my life to enable me to deal with the Song of Songs, and that was a mature, passionate, and deep love. That occurred in my forty- seventh year, when I met my wife and proposed the night that I met her. Although this sounds much like a romance novel, it continues to this day. I come to the Song of Songs with full knowledge of the sacred, spiritual, and sensual awareness of human love in a covenantal relationship. The imagery presented in words is so magnificent that my concepts become realized immediately, and yet one line produces many works. Some of the pieces in this volume were produced in America and some in the Holy Land and span years, not months. This volume contains only a portion of what the Song of Songs has inspired me to create. More can be seen online at www.RatnerMuseum.com.

Phillip Ratner

Also by Shefa Gold

TORAH JOURNEYS: THE INNER PATH
TO THE PROMISED LAND
by **Rabbi Shefa Gold**

Hailed as one of the best Jewish books of 2006 by Beliefnet, and designated "the first Jewish Renewal Torah commentary" by the *New Jersey Jewish News*, **Torah Journeys** transforms the weekly Torah portion into a tool for spiritual growth.

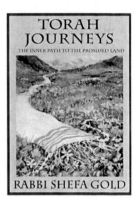

Jewish tradition divides the Five Books of Moses into 54 portions. Following the weekly Torah portion, readers are challenged to think about the Torah in terms of their own lives, and are guided to implement their own spiritual and personal growth. Week by week, **Torah Journeys** makes the Torah personal, and the personal holy.

From each portion, Shefa Gold creates a blessing, a challenge and an original practice for reflection and personal transformation. **Torah Journeys** is an inspiring guide to exploring the landscape of Scripture... and recognizing that landscape as the story of your life.

"Journeying through Torah is a way of sanctifying my own Life's path. Though each of our paths is unique, we travel together through the same shared text."

—From **Torah Journeys**

Available at bookstores and at TorahJourneys.com

"Reb Shefa takes you into the House of Study of the heart and the soul and in this way engages the sacred creativity of the spirit. Reading her Torah teachings one becomes attuned to the voice of the Shekhinah, the feminine aspect of God which brings needed healing to our wounded world."

Reb Zalman Schachter-Shalomi
co-author of *Jewish With Feeling*

"A remarkable book of profound depth. It has taught me much, drawing as the author does from the wells of different faith traditions in her life. Rabbi Shefa Gold is adept at teaching us how to grow spiritually using the Torah as the inexhaustible source. Please read this book if you too want to grow."

Archbishop Emeritus Desmond Tutu

"If you dare be addressed by God — read it.
If you dare be transformed by God — practice it."

Rabbi Rami Shapiro
Author of *The Divine Feminine*

"Even old places and familiar texts we thought we knew come alive again in this book of substance and deep spiritual refreshment. Here experience takes precedence over tired and literal dogmatic pronouncements and life comes alive again."

Theologian Matthew Fox
author of *A New Reformation: Creation Spirituality and the Transformation of Christianity*

"Rabbi Gold opens each Torah portion in profound, new ways, pointing the way for us to find the Torah's most usable blessings, spiritual challenges, and sustainable practices for our own journeys. In *Torah Journeys*, Torah becomes a mirror for our lives and a tool for personal transformation."

Rabbi Tirzah Firestone
author of *The Receiving: Reclaiming Jewish Women's Wisdom* and *With Roots in Heaven: One Woman's Passionate Journey Into The Heart of Her Faith*

Printed in the United States
210808BV00001B/7/P